R. STEPHENSON & SONS,

**Builders and Contractors, Joiners and Cabinet Makers,
Repairs to Property.**

Kell's Lane Joinery Works, LOW FELL.

PLUMBING WORK O 1st X AND REPAIRS.

*Sectional Huts, Bungalows, and
Greenhouses Built to Order.*

P FRONTS AND FITTINGS. OFFICE FITTINGS,

LESS POLES AND INSTALLATIONS COMPLETE.

BEROID FOR FLAT ROOFS A SPECIALITY.
ROCK ASHPHALTE FOR ROOFS.
TEL: GATESHEAD **192.**

2

MARTHA SIMM & SONS,

MANUFACTURERS OF

harcoal, Moulders' Blacking,

Coal Dust, Plumbago, &c., . .

4, NUN'S LANE, GATESHEAD.

GATESHEAD
A Pictorial History

Gateshead, *c.*1835

GATESHEAD
A Pictorial History

Robert Woodhouse

Phillimore

1992

Published by
PHILLIMORE & CO. LTD.,
Shopwyke Hall, Chichester, Sussex

ISBN 0 85033 825 5

Printed and bound in Great Britain by
BIDDLES LTD.,
Guildford, Surrey

List of Illustrations

Frontispiece: Gateshead, *c.*1835

Buildings
1. Gateshead monastery site, 1823
2. Gateshead Town Hall
3. Ornamental detail from the Town Hall clock
4. Statue and ornamental stonework of the Town Hall
5. Goat's head in the Town Hall
6. Council Engineering Services Department
7. Engineering Department, columns
8. Shipley Art Gallery
9. Statue, Shipley Art Gallery
10. Education Department offices
11. Bell tower of the Education Department offices
12. St Mary's church and Tyne Bridge
13. St Mary's church, interior
14. St John's church
15. St Cuthbert's church
16. Victoria Road Methodist church
17. Saltwell Wesleyan Methodist chapel
18. Underhill, Kells Lane
19. Gateshead Youth Industries Workshop
20. Sheriff Hill Hall

High Street
21. Shop premises, nos. 117-121
22. Section of High Street, 1836
23. High Street, February 1939
24. High Street, early 1900s
25. High Street, *c.*1910
26. High Street, *c.*1905
27. High Street, early 1900s
28. *Crown Hotel*
29. High Street, February 1960
30. Wesleyan church, High Street West
31. High Street area, June 1971

Riverside Scenes
32. Gateshead, *c.*1835
33. Prospect of Gateshead from across the Tyne, mid-1800s
34. Pipewellgate, 1898
35. Construction work on Gateshead Quay, August 1930
36. Construction work on Gateshead Quay, August 1931
37. Three Tyne bridges
38. Friar's Goose slipway
39. Former Co-op soapworks, Dunston
40. River Police headquarters building
41. Friar's Goose Marina
42. East Gateshead Riverside Park
43. Bensham Road and the Derwentwater Valley

Industrial and Commercial Premises
44. Friar's Goose pumping engine house
45. C.W.S. girls peeling onions at the Pelaw works, 1901
46. Demolition of Rank Hovis Mill, December 1983
47. W. H. Smith premises
48. Team Valley area before development of the trading estate
49. Team Valley Trading Estate
50. Team Valley, a study in straight lines
51. Tyneside Peeled Potatoes Ltd.
52. Clarke Chapman's Victoria Works
53. Clarke Chapman's assembly shop

Transport
54. A steam engine and trailer
55. Tram in the early 1900s
56. Heworth tram terminus
57. Gateshead tram staff
58. List of tram fares
59. Staff of Gateshead trams, 1940
60. The Wellington Street approach to Gateshead railway station, 1920s
61. Railway bridge, West Street
62. North-Eastern Railway goods station
63. North-Eastern Railway staff, *c.*1910
64. A 'Big City Traffic Hold-up', 9 July 1951
65. The first section of the Gateshead-Felling bypass in May 1959

Schools and Schooldays
66. Gateshead Grammar school
67. The Health School on Joicey Road
68. Kelvin Grove school
69. John Kelly outside Prior Street junior school
70. Pupils at Prior Street school, 1914

71. Pupils at Prior Street school, 1927-28
72. Miss Smith's class at Corpus Christi school
73. Carol Lytollis returns home after school, 1950
74. Brighton Avenue school pupils, 1909
75. Alexandra Road schools
76. Pupils in the yard of Whitehall Road school, early 1950s

Street Scenes and Housing Developments
77. Bowl Alley Bank
78. Pipewellgate, 1886
79. St Mary's church
80. Church Street, 1920s
81. Bridge Street, 1924
82. Church Street, 1930
83. Bottle Bank
84. Amen Corner
85. Durham Road, Low Fell, c.1900
86. Pipewellgate, 1927
87. Shop premises, Saltwell Road
88. Pine Street
89. Demolition work behind West Street
90. Terraced properties, Derwentwater Road
91. Avenue Road
92. Belle Vue Bank
93. Beacon Lough estate, 1952
94. Lobley Hill district
95. Easdale Gardens, Lyndhurst estate
96. Stone arch on Sheriff Hill

Saltwell Park
97. Salt Well
98. Saltwell Park, 1920
99. Saltwell Tower
100. Saltwell Towers, interior
101. An exhibit from the mansion in Saltwell Park
102. Carvings in the mansion
103. Golden goat from the *Goat Inn*
104. Mulberry tree hall stand
105. Kiosk from the North East Coast Exhibition in Saltwell Park
106. The drinking fountain
107. Saltwell Park lake, 1904
108. Saltwell Park bandstand
109. Model yacht club members at Saltwell Park, c.1900
110. Carol and Eileen Lytollis, 1948
111. Brenda Lamb at Saltwell Park, 1948
112. Group photograph by the lake, 1949

Local People
113. William Errington Kelly and his wife
114. Sabina Kelly and sons, 1906
115. George and John Kelly, 1909
116. Bina Kelly, Willa Kelly and Bina Nuttall in 1922

117. Willa Kelly with family, 1934
118. Bina and Willa Kelly, 1935
119. Bernard Kelly, 1934
120. The Kelly family, Ravensworth, 1936
121. Ravensworth Castle
122. Gateway to Ravensworth Castle
123. Walter Nuttall, 1938
124. Sabina and William Errington Kelly, 1939
125. Willa Kelly, August 1938
126. Atlas Stone football team, 1930s
127. Jack and Willa Lamb on their wedding day, 1942
128. Brenda Lamb, 1946
129. 'The Jolly Boys', 1947
130. William Errington Kelly, 1950
131. Brenda Lamb and Margaret Taylor at a dancing class, 1951
132. Local people opposite the Cooperative Society premises in Whitehall Road, 1951
133. A family day out at Ravensworth, 1952
134. Hearses in Brussel Street, 1955
135. Alexander Gillies, Mayor of Gateshead
136. Shipcote Villa, c.1900
137. No. 2 Shipcote Villa, c.1900
138. The library, no. 2 Shipcote Villa, c.1900
139. The drawing room, no. 2 Shipcote Villa
140. Helen and Henzel Dance, c.1910
141. Brake cart and the Dance family, c.1900
142. Local folk on a family outing
143. Home Guard and despatch riders, Burt Terrace
144. The Rev. Mr. Rhodes addressing the lads, 1906
145. Boys Brigade members at Ravensworth, 1909
146. Harrison's Slipway staff before the Cutty Sark race

Social Life
147. Postcard from Gateshead, 1933
148. Essoldo Cinema
149. Palace Cinema
150. Coatsworth Picture Hall
151. Rex Cinema, 1939
152. Regulars in their local pub, Saltmeadows area
153. *Beacon Hotel* in June 1962
154. *Norwood Hotel*, 1965
155. *Plough Inn* at Deckham, December 1967

Local Events
156. Battle of Friar's Goose, 1832
157. Pitmen encamped, 8 May 1832
158. Newton Street celebrations, 1902
159. Bonfire under construction at Shadon's Hill, 1902
160. A local army parade, 1906
161. V.E. party in Westbourne Avenue, May 1945

162. Local children celebrate the coronation of Queen Elizabeth II on 2 June 1953
163. Celebrations at Corpus Christi school, 1953
164. Festival Queen at Corpus Christi school, 1953
165. Youngsters in fancy dress, Corpus Christi school on Empire Day, 1953
166. Councillor Bob Rudge at the Dispensary building, 12 October 1982
167. Dunston end of the Garden Festival site
168. The pavilion, National Garden Festival, 1990
169. Ferris wheel, National Garden Festival

170. Monorail and 'Red Army', National Garden Festival
171. Coal staiths, National Garden Festival
172. Brendan Foster at Gateshead Riverside Bowl, 1975
173. Schweppes International cross country team, 25 November 1978
174. Jill Hunter after the Trophy Run at Gateshead, 1984
175. American athletes Ed Moses and Florence Joyner at the Gateshead stadium, 1988
176. Shopping malls in the Metro Centre
177. The Metro Centre

Acknowledgements

The north-east is noted for team efforts on the sporting scene, and this book extends the tradition into the world of books, for a considerable number of people have played an invaluable part in its production.

Dave Morrell copied original prints and provided a range of practical advice and comments throughout the preparation of the materials. My son, John Woodhouse, was of considerable assistance in researching aspects of the work and in typing the text.

Photographs have been drawn from many sources and I am indebted to a number of people for their cooperation in tracking down and allowing reproduction of these prints. Mrs. Brenda Thompson gathered family photographs from relatives who formerly lived in Gateshead and provided background details, Paul Sutherland and colleagues in the *Evening Chronicle* in Newcastle arranged for the use of prints from the newspaper's considerable collection of material from the Gateshead area. Jim Lawson and colleagues at Beamish Hall arranged for the use of prints from their photographic archive and Paul Keenan in the marketing department of the Metro Centre loaned materials illustrating this impressive development. Other photographs are from the private collection of Mr. K. C. Warne of Middlesbrough.

I have received a tremendous amount of advice and assistance from staff in several of Gateshead's civic departments. Tyneside warmth and cooperation has been shown by many people including John Pendlebury of Gateshead planning department, Eileen Carnaffin, the local studies librarian at Gateshead central library, Stan Long and colleagues in the leisure services department and Kris Gray in the public relations department. My grateful thanks are extended to all of them.

A considerable effort has been made to ensure the accuracy of material included in this book which it is hoped will represent and reflect the unique culture that makes up this area of Tyneside.

Illustration Acknowledgements

Robert Woodhouse would like to acknowledge the use of photographs in this book as follows:

Newcastle Chronicle and Journal Ltd., 1-16, 18-29, 31-36, 38-54, 61, 64-68, 77, 78, 80, 82-84, 86-99, 101-6, 146, 148-50, 153-59, 166, 167; Beamish North of England Open Air Museum, 17, 30, 55-59, 63, 74, 75, 100, 108-9, 121, 122, 126, 135-145, 152, 160; R. Woodhouse, 37; Mrs. B. Thompson, 60, 62, 69-73, 76, 110-20, 123-25, 127-34, 161-65; Gateshead libraries and arts department, 79, 81, 85, 151, 168-71; Mr. K. C. Warne, 107, 147; Mr. S. Long, 172-75; Metro Centre photographic files, 176-77.

Introduction

Local government reorganisation in 1974 gave Gateshead Metropolitan Borough status and created a large administrative area with a total population of 211,333. Central Gateshead, with a population of 74,644 in 1981, was the fourth largest town in County Durham. Today most people live in housing developments in the southern suburbs but the original township grew up close to the river bank.

The discovery, in the late 18th and early 19th centuries, of coins and artefacts of possible Roman origin, probably indicates the existence of a small settlement close to the road bridge across the River Tyne. Forts were built at Pons Aelius (Newcastle) on the northern bank and at Whickham, just outside the Gateshead boundary, but any remaining evidence of Roman occupation along the riverside will have disappeared with successive redevelopment schemes.

There is a reference in Bede's *History of the English Church and People* to a monastery at Gateshead under Abbot Utta, in A.D. 653, but its location is unknown and there is no indication that there was a settlement of any size at this time. Another early monastic writer, Symeon of Durham, describes the murder of Walcher, the first Norman Bishop of Durham, in Gateshead in 1080. It was during the late 11th and throughout the 12th centuries that the township grew in size and importance.

Much of the land in the Gateshead area was covered by forest and Bishop Hugh le Puiset (and his successors) spent time at their manor house whilst hunting in the nearby forest areas. In 1164 Bishop le Puiset granted borough rights to his forest and the township seems to have prospered around the southern end of the bridging point across the Tyne. There was a further period of growth for Gateshead during the 14th century, with the beginning of coal-mining operations in 1344, and the construction of wharves at Pipewellgate in 1349. A market had probably been established almost a century earlier, and by the mid-1300s the town had a market on two days a week – Tuesdays and Thursdays. It was also a period of rivalry with Newcastle and attempts were made by Gateshead's northern neighbour to restrict its growing importance. Under this pressure subsequent bishops of Durham lost interest in the town and Bishop Hatfield's survey of 1380 shows that the manor of Gateshead, which had originally been held by the bishop, had been let. Most of the disputes between Newcastle and Gateshead related to the bridge and shipping rights on the Tyne. During the 1400s settlements began to turn in favour of Newcastle.

The development of coalfields in the Gateshead area during the late 15th and early 16th centuries increased the determination of Newcastle's leading citizens to annex their southern neighbour, and on 30 March 1553 annexation became law. Almost a year later, on 2 April 1554, Parliament passed a bill to re-establish the bishopric of Durham and include Gateshead within it. During the 1570s there were further attempts by merchants in Newcastle to gain control of Gateshead and its profitable coal mines. In the face of this renewed challenge the townspeople of Gateshead petitioned strongly against such a move by writing to eminent Parliamentarians and public figures in the capital, and plans for annexation were dropped. The businessmen of Newcastle, however, were not to be denied and Thomas Sutton, Master of the Ordance at Berwick-on-Tweed, used his influence in court circles to arrange for the lease on two of the Bishop of Durham's richest manors to be transferred to commercial interests on the north side of the Tyne. An indication of the business development that followed is shown by the amounts of coal shipments for 1574-75 which amounted to 56,487 tons, and 1677-78 when shipments totalled 602,610 tons. During this century the population of Gateshead more than doubled. Trade and commerce was disrupted by Scottish incursions during the Civil War period. Sir Thomas Liddell's coal mines were damaged during fighting in 1640 and there was further damage and disruption to the Gateshead area during the siege of Newcastle in 1644.

By the 1680s Gateshead's fortunes were in decline. Accessible coal seams were almost worked out and a lack of pumping machinery prevented exploitation of deeper reserves. It was the mid-18th century before technical progress in mines and the development of other industries such as iron-making and glass manufacture revived the town's economic prospects.

Transportation of coal from pithead to riverside staiths caused serious damage to the local landscape. Packhorses were first used to carry coal but these were replaced, probably in the 15th century, by horse and ox-drawn wheeled vehicles called wains. Wooden rails were probably in use on Tyneside by the 1630s and in 1663 Sir Thomas Liddell built the Ravensworth wagonway to run coal vehicles along the west side of the Team Valley to a staith on the River Team at Dunston.

Ships were under construction on the south side of the Tyne during the 17th century, and although members of Newcastle guilds tried to retain a monopoly of the shipbuilding industry it continued on a very limited scale in the Gateshead area until recent years. Coal-mining and shipbuilding led to a demand for rope, and a ropemakers guild was established in Newcastle during 1648. By the early 18th century ropemaking was also underway on the south side of the River Tyne. The Haggie family was to the forefront in running a ropeworks at Southgate, and in 1840 two wire ropeworks were opened in the Teams area by R. S. Newall and Co. and Dixon Corbitt. Other industries also experienced periods of prosperity and depression. Grindstones had been quarried from fells to the south of Gateshead since the Middle Ages, and after a period of inactivity in the early 1700s, quarries were reopened to provide grindstones until the emphasis changed to building stone in the 1830s. There is reference to milling at Gateshead in the late 12th century and the town's importance as a mining centre for this area of County Durham continued into the 18th century. The manufacture of pottery was underway by the 14th century but then lapsed until it was re-established in the town during the mid-1700s. John Carr set up premises at Carr Hill in the 1740s and some thirty years later Paul Jackson opened the Sheriff Hill pottery on a site alongside Old Durham Road.

Much of the industrial development of the mid-18th century was in the hands of local families who extended their business interests to include potteries, ironworks, and brickyards at locations such as Hillgate, South Shore, Pipewellgate and Teams. Numbered among these industries were several noxious trades such as a whale blubber boilery and glue factories, which made the town an unpleasant environment. Contemporary writers were unimpressed by the locality and

Dr. Samuel Johnson (1709-84) described Gateshead as 'a dirty lane leading to Newcastle'.

Industrial expansion continued into the 19th century and the increasing population in the towns of the north-east produced serious social problems. Greater numbers of elderly and infirm people needed assistance, and poor housing and sanitary conditions required large amounts of capital expenditure. Faced with an increase in amounts levied from poor rates of £568 in 1780 to £4,500 in 1820, ratepayers protested strongly and during the summer of 1821 new rules for relief were introduced (one regulation related to able-bodied males who were to be offered relief in return for stone-breaking). As a consequence, expenditure on relief fell to £3,040 in 1822.

Legislative changes during the 1830s transformed most aspects of Gateshead's political and administrative activity. The Reform Act of 1832 resulted in the town gaining its first Member of Parliament. Three years later the town's first council was elected, and in 1836 Gateshead was placed at the centre of a Poor Law Union. The development of the railway boosted local industrial output and attracted more workers to the town, with the result that Gateshead's population increased from 15,000 during the 1820s to almost 20,000 by 1840.

Housing conditions and sanitary arrangements were not maintained and, in common with other north-eastern towns, Gateshead suffered an outbreak of cholera during the 1830s. The appalling housing conditions were highlighted in a 'Report to the General Board of Health ... on a Preliminary Inquiry into ... the Borough of Gateshead, 1850'. The inspecting engineer, Robert Rawlinson, reported 'ruinous brickwork ... rotten timber ... and an appearance of general decay'. Superior residences, close to Hillgate, which were being let as tenements, had become overcrowded and suffered from dampness and all the obvious signs of dereliction.

For many years Gateshead was surrounded by landed estates, and it was not until after 1860 that sectors of land became available for housing development. During the 1860s and '70s land was released from the Park estate to the east of the town and the Shipcote estate on the west. Provision of small terraced houses for workers soon outstripped the increase in population, which had risen from 33,589 in 1861 to 65,845 in 1881. This situation was reversed during the 1880s as the population increase exceeded the number of houses available, but from the late 1880s there was a second building boom. Houses now became larger, having three rooms at ground level and four on the first floor; an extended rear wing contained a kitchen, scullery and back yard.

The residents of the town could find relief from the overcrowded conditions by walking to nearby vantage points such as Sheriff Hill (538 ft. above sea level) which gave fine views of the surrounding countryside. The southern sector of the town also includes the 58-acre Saltwell Park, which was landscaped for public use by W. B. Kemp from Birkenhead in 1877. An expanse of lawn swept down to a large lake and original features included a long terrace of flowers, a secluded sunken rose garden and a hedged enclosure with an open-air draughtboard. Saltwell Towers, which stands close to the lake, was designed in 1856 and constructed during 1860-71 for the Tyneside glass manufacturer, William Wailes. The red brickwork of the main structure was highlighted by yellow and black materials, whilst turrets, chimneys and battlements added a touch of Victorian grandeur. The interior included extravagant fittings and furniture but sadly these have long since been removed. During the immediate post-war years this fine 19th-century mansion was used as a local and industrial museum, but it now stands unused and in a poor state of repair.

Sir Joseph Wilson Swan, scientist and inventor of the incandescent lamp, the carbon print photograph and the cellulose filament, lived at Gateshead for 14 years. His house, Underhill, on Kells Lane in the Low Fell district, was the first to be lit by electric lamps, for it was here in 1878 that Swan found the key to the problem of the incandescent lamp. He discovered that carbon sealed in a vacuum did not waste away. He demonstrated his invention to the Newcastle Chemical Society on 18 December. During the first two years of experiments, members of Swan's household carried out the delicate work of forming the filament for carbonisation. In 1881 German glassblowers were employed and the commercial manufacture of the lamp began at Benwell on the outskirts of Newcastle.

During the second half of the 19th century a number of large residences were built for businessmen and industrialists on the southern edge of Gateshead. These include Belle Vue House, Belle Vue Bank and Ravenshill, Durham Road. Many of them were built in the Italianate style, such as Whinney House, Durham Road, which was built in 1864 for the coal-mining Joicey family. This imposing building, with square tower and stable block has been used as Whinney House hospital in recent years. A short distance away, to the north, Heathfield House has a triumphal arch gateway. Built in 1856 for the town clerk, it is now used as council flats, with a school in the grounds.

The growth of the town during the early 20th century can be plotted in the names of the Gateshead Fell area: Kitchener Terrace, Baden-Powell Terrace and Methuen Terrace recall heroes of the South African war of 1899-1901. During the years before the First World War the problem of overcrowding was being tackled. The Housing Act of 1909 gave increased powers to sanitary inspectors and allowed closing orders on tenement properties. Areas such as Pipewellgate, Bottle Bank, Church Walk and Barn Close were improved as demolition orders were served in greater numbers.

During the 1900s the town's only remaining colliery, Redheugh, increased the number of its employees; but alarming signs began to show in other industries. John Abbot and Co., iron manufacturers, closed in 1909 and I. C. Johnson's Portland cement works was on the point of closure. During 1910 the North Eastern Railway Works moved most of its work to Darlington and employment levels at the United Alkali Company fell from a total of 1,200 in 1899 to 1,030 in 1908 and future prospects were bleak. Increased demand for munitions during the First World War raised employment levels in Gateshead, but in 1919 the industrial depression returned, continuing until the late 1920s, with the relocation of the chemical industry on Teeside and the closure of remaining collieries.

Many houses in the centre of Gateshead had become unfit for habitation during the war, and in the 1920s council housing was built in the Sheriff Hill/Carr Hill and Old Ford areas. Private estates developed along Durham Road and Low Fell and these schemes continued into the 1930s. Further council housing was provided at Field House, Wrekenton, Lobley Hill and Deckham Hall. Private developments were completed at Dryden Road, Chowdene and Harlow Green, but there was still an overall shortage of housing in the town. The clearance of riverside properties was underway in the 1920s as part of the programme of work associated with construction of the Tyne Bridge. The Housing Act of 1930 provided greater legal powers to deal with slum housing, and large scale demolition schemes were implemented during the early 1930s. Pipewellgate, Hillgate, Bridge Street and Church Street were included among sectors of the town that were subjected to compulsory purchase and then demolished. New housing did not keep pace, however, and in 1936 a national housing survey showed Gateshead to be the next worse county borough in England, with 15.8 per cent of its population living in overcrowded conditions.

The depressing atmosphere that had settled over Gateshead during the inter-war years proved difficult to transform and in 1934 J. B. Priestley described the town as 'nothing better than a huge dingy dormitory'. A lack of private investment was the underlying problem for depressed industrial areas at this time, and in 1934 the government appointed a Commissioner for Special Areas to investigate remedial schemes. By August 1935 plans were in hand for the establishment of trading estates, and one was allocated for the north-east. North Eastern Trading Estates Limited was formed on 18 May 1936 and the site selected for the estate was the Team Valley on the west side of Gateshead. During August 1936 construction work began, with about seven hundred acres of land being stabilised using millions of tons of colliery waste. Plans for the site were prepared by W. G. Holford and included the canalisation and cleansing of the River Team. A wide road ran from north to south and other parallel routes formed a network of long, straight avenues.

The Team Valley Trading Estate was formally opened by King George VI on 22 February 1939 and construction work continued during the war years. Most buildings were long, low brick structures; the best examples were probably the factory for Sigmund Pumps in Queensway, designed by F. R. S. Yorke in 1948, and the Durham China Company's premises in Earlsway, completed in 1951. In spite of changes of ownership, additions and alterations to many of the original buildings, the estate retains its original plan.

A riverside sector of land in east Gateshead, the Saltmeadows, was bought in 1936, but it was not until the early 1960s that a 35-acre site was prepared for industrial use, at a cost of £100,000. By 1966 most of the area had been leased for construction of small factories and depots.

As the northern bank of the Tyne emerged as a major business and commercial centre during the 19th and 20th centuries, a number of bridging points were constructed. The Tyne Bridge, built by Dorman Long and Co. Ltd., was opened by King George V in 1928. The roadway is suspended 84 ft. above the river from a gigantic, graceful arch which contains 4,000 tons of steel, while the bridge's foundations are nearly 70 ft. below water level. At a lower level, and upstream from the Tyne Bridge, is the Swing Bridge, which was completed in 1876. It lies at approximately the same crossing point as a Roman bridge, a medieval bridge, and the nine-arched stone bridge of 1772-81. The iron structure – some 280 ft. long – is still operated by its original hydraulic system, with power from electric pumps and includes a central control tower and lighthouse.

The High Level Bridge demonstrates the brilliant engineering skill of Robert Stephenson. Construction of this six-arched crossing, which carries a rail deck on the upper level and road traffic below, took four years (1845-49). It was opened by Queen Victoria. The bridge represents one of the first civil engineering works to employ James Nasmyth's steam hammer (for driving the piles carrying the piers) and, along with the Royal Border Bridge at Berwick-upon-Tweed, it formed the last of the major rail links between London and Edinburgh. King Edward VII Railway

Bridge was built in 1906 to carry through traffic on the east coast mainline some 112 ft. above the river. The Metro Bridge was completed in 1980 and carries Tyneside's new rapid transit system across the river in three 1,200 ft. long sections.

Gas and water mains were used as structural members of the Redheugh Bridge of 1871, which was replaced 30 years later by a bridge incorporating unusual Pennsylvanian trusses in its four spans. This structure was in turn replaced by a modern road bridge in the early 1980s.

Other bridges in the vicinity are the road bridge at Scotswood and the railway bridge which dates from the last century and replaced the first railway crossing. Her Majesty Queen Elizabeth II continued a royal tradition stretching back more than 140 years when she opened the Blaydon Bridge on 1 December 1990. It was the sixth royal opening of a Tyneside river crossing, a tradition which began when Queen Victoria opened the High Level Bridge in 1849.

Clearance of the small, original riverside settlement began in the early 1900s and continued into the 1950s. Although the population of Gateshead was declining during this period, a greater number of families needed housing, and during the 1950s the decision was made to build tower blocks and to extend housing developments across the borough boundary. In 1954 the Wrekenton Neighbourhood Unit of 1,372 houses was completed and the first families were rehoused in the Leam Lane estate. The first multi-storey block on Tyneside, at Barn Close, was completed in August 1955 and three other blocks were constructed on the same site. More multi-storey housing was opened at Regent Court in 1958, Bensham in 1962 and Chandless in 1962-63. The shortcomings of such schemes led to an alternative approach; a 'village' concept, which resulted in the St Cuthbert's Village and Clasper Village developments.

During the last 30 years much of the town centre has been cleared to accommodate 'relief' roads, dual carriageways, flyovers, roundabouts and underpasses. Schemes such as the Felling bypass (1960), the Gateshead highway (1961), and Western bypass (1971), have provided direct access to Newcastle by the bridging points across the River Tyne, but they leave little of the early township intact.

Closer to the original heart of the township there are a number of public buildings of considerable interest. Shipley Art Gallery stands near the north-east corner of Saltwell Park. Named after Joseph Shipley, a local solicitor who died in 1909, it was opened six years after his death as part of a civic group of buildings which include municipal offices and a public library. Its impressive architectural features include a colonnaded entrance surmounted by two colossal groups of statuary illustrating the tuition of youth in the arts and sciences. The public library was completed in 1925 and includes aspects of design work from the art gallery. A red-brick extension was added during the early 1970s.

Many of Gateshead's churches were built during the 19th century and a number have been demolished in the last 20 years. Among those that survive, albeit adapted for alternative use, are Holy Trinity on the High Street and St Mary's, which occupies a position overlooking the Tyne in the shadow of Tyne Bridge. Sections of the Holy Trinity church building date from the 13th century, when it was a chapel for a medieval hospital; it was adapted as a parish church during the 19th century. Its position on the High Street made the building an ideal venue for social activity, and in 1980, when it was no longer needed as a place of worship, a careful conversion scheme was carried out. Important architectural features were preserved in the re-styled building. Part of it continues to be used as a church whilst the other section is used as the Trinity Community Centre.

St Mary's church dates mostly from the 14th century although the west tower was added in the 18th century. Interior furnishings included 17th-century pews and chancel stalls, a baroque-style cartouche under the tower, and monuments to former townspeople who died in foreign parts. Earlier buildings on the site had been badly damaged in fires; the first in 1080, when Bishop Walcher was murdered and his church destroyed, and again in 1854 during the Great Fire of Newcastle when a nearby chemical works exploded showering rocks and debris upon the church roof. On the night of 19 October 1979 St Mary's was again badly damaged by fire, and for the next 10 years it remained as an eyesore on high ground alongside the Tyne Bridge. The church was deconsecrated and stayed empty and unused as successive plans for conversion into flats, a shopping centre, a charity centre, and restaurant failed to materialise. It was acquired by the North East Civic Trust which transferred ownership to Phillips Fine Art Auctioneers. They arranged for the church interior to be converted into salesrooms and offices. The church was formally handed over to the company in November 1990 and further work on the project included the restyling of the churchyard in order to create an access road to the premises.

Further evidence of Gateshead's re-emergence as an important member of the Tyne and Wear conurbation has been seen in three recent projects. During the 1980s Gateshead Stadium became a major venue for international athletics events. It also provided a home base for the town's football club, which has experienced fluctuating fortunes since its formation from the South Shields club in 1930. Since 1990 the club has played in the G.M. Vauxhall Conference League and recent sponsorship deals have raised hopes that League football will soon be played at the impressive all-seater stadium.

During the early 1980s derelict riverside land covering 115 acres was converted into Britain's largest out-of-town shopping complex – the Metro Centre. It was opened in October 1986 by Nicholas Ridley, Secretary of State for the Environment, and represented a £250 million investment by Cameron Hall Ltd. Facilities include a 10-screen cinema and a bowling centre, in addition to the 1.5 million square feet of retail space. This prestigious development on Gateshead's western side also provides employment for more than 5,500 local people.

Another large tract of derelict industrial land in the Team Valley district was chosen as the setting for the 1990 National Garden Festival. Opened by the Princess Royal in May 1990, it included more than 100 gardens or garden features. These ranged from a wetlands garden, devised by the Northumberland Wildlife Trust and sponsored by British Coal, to a display of municipal gardening from Harrogate with a heavy emphasis on hanging baskets and summer bedding plants. The Durham County Council garden included a large central pavilion in the form of a striped medieval jousting tent. It served to commemorate the fact that County Durham has been known as the land of the Prince Bishops since the medieval period. The northern sector of this site, which sloped down to the River Tyne, contained a number of unusual features, such as a large turbine fountain, a turf maze, and a classical Japanese garden. Most impressive of all, however, was the restored 19th-century wooden coaling staiths, where colliers were loaded for the journey to London.

Bibliography

Books
Barbey, M. F., *Civil Engineering Heritage* (1981)
Dewdney, J. C. (ed.), *Durham County and City with Teesside* (1970)
Fraser, C., and Emsley, K., *Northumbria* (1989)
Hardy, Clive, *Tyneside since 1900* (1988)
Manders, F. W. D., *A History of Gateshead* (1973)
McCord, N., *North East England, the Region's Development (1760-1960)* (1979)
McCord, N., *North-East History from the Air* (1991)
Pevsner, Nikolaus, *The Buildings of England: County Durham* (1983)
Pocock, D., and Norris, R., *A History of County Durham* (1990)
Rippon, A., *Great Soccer Clubs of the North East* (1981)
Thorold, Henry, *County Durham: A Shell Guide* (1980)

Articles
Various articles and newspaper reports from the files stored in Gateshead library.
Publicity material supplied by the Marketing Department of the Metro Centre and Gateshead Leisure Services.
Material supplied from the archive materials stored at Beamish Hall.

Buildings

1. The site of Gateshead monastery in 1823. The earliest mention of the monastery appears in Bede's *History of the English Church and People* (A.D. 653). Holy Trinity church and community centre buildings now occupy this area.

2. Gateshead Town Hall on West Street. Built between 1868-70, it was designed in the Venetian Renaissance style by John Johnstone. The balustraded parapet includes a central statue (see plate 4).

3. *(right)* Ornamental detail from the top of the Town Hall clock, showing the weathervane and finely carved cupola.

4. *(below)* Statue and ornamental stonework on the upper roof level of the Town Hall, with stone balustrading on either side.

5. *(below right)* A carving of a goat's head on Gateshead Town Hall. It is suggested that in earlier times goats roamed the high ground to the south-east of Gateshead and this accounts for the appearance of a number of carvings and statues in the town.

6. Currently in use as the Council Engineering Services Department building, it was opened as the town library in 1885. A new library was opened on Prince Consort Road in 1925.

7. Columns of the Council Engineering Services Department at second-floor level, on either side of the central section.

8. Shipley Art Gallery on Prince Consort Road. Completed
between 1914-17, it formed part of a set of civic buildings
planned for a site to the south of the town. Although the library
and education offices were completed during the 1920s, other
buildings (including a theatre) were not built since the
depression of the 1930s curtailed the original plans.

9. Statue at the Shipley Art Gallery in Prince Consort Road.
Seated stone figures top both side piers of the Corinthian-style
portico.

10.   Education Department offices on Prince Consort Road situated between the Shipley Art Gallery and the library.

11.   Bell tower and weathervane of the Education Department offices.

12. St Mary's church and Tyne Bridge – two of the town's major landmarks. Badly damaged by fire in 1855 and 1979, St Mary's has been reopened by Phillips Fine Art Auctioneers as a saleroom and offices. The Tyne Bridge was completed between 1925-28, with steelwork by Dorman Long Ltd. At the time of its opening the bridge was the largest of its kind in the world.

13. Interior of St Mary's church showing the chancel arch and pews, which date from 1634. The ends of the pews were decorated with strapwork and carved foliage; the chancel stalls were similar but dated from 1695.

14. St John's church, Sheriff Hill, from a print of 1828. The church had only been completed a few years earlier (1824-25) and the area retains a rural aspect.

15. St Cuthbert's church, Bensham Road, seen from Hall Terrace, built in the late 1840s and largely Norman in style. This photograph highlights the early English tower at the west end. The chancel was refitted between 1885-1902.

16. Victoria Road Methodist church and Sunday School. The church and the school were established in 1882; this photograph was taken 103 years later and shows the high rise development which was a feature of Gateshead's growth during the 1950s and '60s.

17. Saltwell Wesleyan Methodist chapel was situated on the corner of Rawlivey Road and Faraday Grove. The photograph dates from the 1940s.

18. Underhill on Kells Lane is the former residence of Sir Joseph Swan who invented the electric light bulb on these premises. His laboratory was the first to be lit by an electric bulb and his invention was demonstrated in 1879 at a meeting of the Literary and Philosophical Society. The building is now used as a nursing home.

19. The upper floor of Gateshead Youth Industries Workshop, Public Baths and Laundries.

20. A local stately home, Sheriff Hill Hall, photographed in the summer of 1962. The building was threatened with demolition in the early 1960s. Part of the building, however, now has listed building status and is still standing.

High Street

21.   Gateshead High Street, showing shop premises nos. 117-21. Preston's, to the left of centre, was a brush works. All of these properties were demolished in the early 1920s, before work started on the Tyne Bridge. They were situated opposite the modern Tesco store and north of Gateshead post office.

22.   A drawing of a section of Gateshead High Street in 1836. Harrison's premises housed cooperage and this accounts for the assortment of barrels and bowls.

23.   Gateshead High Street pictured in February 1939. During the town's Brewster sessions it was described as 'a blot on the town' but in this photograph tramlines, overhead cables and shop frontages are highlighted by street lighting to give an attractive night-time perspective.

24. Gateshead High Street looking north in the early 1900s. The Queens Theatre is visible on the left, and ornamental supports for tram wires brighten the centre of the wide thoroughfare.

25. Gateshead High Street, c.1910, with several horse-drawn vehicles and a single tram in the distance.

26.   An absence of traffic along this lower section of the town's main thoroughfare and the elegant fashions of several people on the west side could indicate that the picture was taken on a sunny Sunday afternoon, *c*.1905.

27. Tall commercial premises on the left form a contrast with the smaller shops across the road in this photograph taken in the early years of the 20th century. Apart from a small number of horse-drawn vehicles, the street is remarkably free from traffic.

28. *Crown Hotel* on the High Street photographed in April 1960. King Charles I stayed at an earlier *Crown Hotel* during a visit to the town in 1646. This building was demolished during the late 1960s and on 10 May 1968 press reports stated that the site had been acquired as a car-park for the post office.

29.   The High Street pictured in February 1960. Work is underway to fix huge steel central supports for the railway bridge.

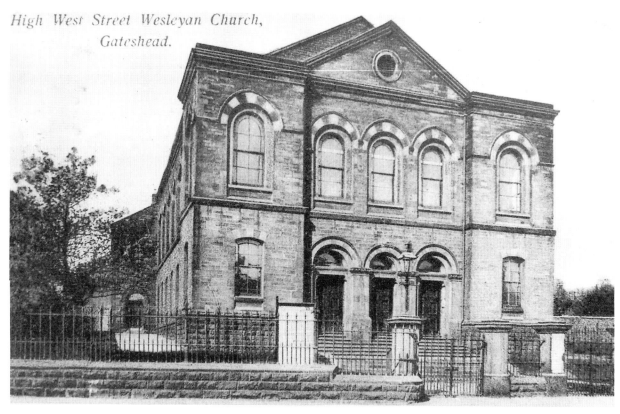

High West Street Wesleyan Church, Gateshead.

30. Wesleyan church, High Street West, photographed in 1905.

31. Most of the original properties along the High Street had gone by June 1971, the date of this picture. Swinburne Street is seen on the left and the curved superstructure of the Tyne Bridge appears above the skyline in the middle distance.

Riverside Scenes

32. Gateshead, *c*.1835. This view from the Moot Hall shows the town from the Tyne to Sheriff Hill. The only public buildings are the parish church and the ruins of the ancient chapel. It is possible to pick out the developing High Street and West Street areas in the centre of the picture.

33.   A view from the mid-1800s looking across the Tyne towards Gateshead. Sailing vessels line the riverside which is crowded with warehouses, whilst St Mary's church dominates the high ground above the river.

34.   Pipewellgate in 1898 when Brett's premises housed a glassworks. The sector of riverside land known as Pipewellgate was for many years the main centre of Gateshead. It ran from Redheugh to the old Tyne Bridge (now the Swing Bridge). The Ordnance Survey map of 1858 shows a collection of noxious industries including chemical works situated within this area. 'Pipe' in the name may be a reference to pipes carrying water.

35. Construction work continues on Gateshead Quay on 29 August 1930 in spite of a heatwave.

36. Construction work on the new Gateshead Quay in late August 1931.

37.   Three Tyne bridges photographed from the air: Tyne Bridge, 1925-28 (to the right), Swing Bridge, 1868-76 (in the centre) and High Level Bridge, 1845-49 (on the left). The commercial heart of Newcastle spreads down to the northern riverbank, whilst warehousing and storage facilities cover the southern sector of Gateshead's river frontage.

38. Friar's Goose Slipway photographed in 1963. Most of the work at the yard was concerned with ship repairs and refitting.

39. The derelict former Co-op soapworks at Dunstan stands out above the site of the National Garden Festival on the riverbank. The building could not be demolished or altered since it had listed building status.

40. The river police headquarters building at Pipewellgate. Press reports of 1910 suggest that construction work for the premises was underway by this date.

41. The Felling shore of Friar's Goose marina pictured in June 1979.

42. East Gateshead Riverside Park showing the remains of Friar's Goose pumping station. This 68-acre site was reclaimed in the early 1970s at a cost of £110,000.

43. Bensham Road and Derwentwater Valley looking across the West Teams and past Dunston power station towards Blaydon. This view of the river landscape was opened up after demolition work in the early 1980s and before construction of the Metro Centre.

44. Friar's Goose pumping house had one of the most powerful engines on the Tyne in the early 19th century. It was used to draw off water from the main seam of the Tyne main colliery. In November 1841 a fire in nearby screens threatened to destroy pumps and the engine house itself.

45. A photograph taken in 1901 shows Cooperative Wholesale Society girls peeling onions at the Pelaw works. Until the Cooperative Society began to develop premises in the late 1890s Pelaw was a green-field site. Construction of a drug factory was followed by a dry saltery, furniture and shirt factories.

46. Demolition of the Rank Hovis Mill in December 1983. Built in 1931, it had a capacity for storing 20,000 tonnes of grain or flour.

47. W. H. Smith and Son brick-built premises alongside the wooden frontage of Moffatt Bros. Ltd.

48. Views of the Team Valley area before development of the trading estate. (*Top*) From the east looking across Saltwell and Sheriff Hill to Lobley Hill. (*Bottom*) From the south-west with Birtley on the left.

LOBLEY HILL

TO GATESHEAD & NEWCASTLE

L.N.E.R. MAIN LINE

PHOTO-PHILIPSON

RAVENSWORTH

NEWCASTLE

TO NEWCASTLE ON TYNE

L.N.E.R. LONDON TO NEWCASTLE

TO GT. NORTH RD ½ MILE

49.   Team Valley Trading Estate showing Martins Bank premises and adjacent post office. North Eastern Trading Estates Ltd. was formed on 18 May 1936 and development of the 700-acre site got underway in August of that year. The trading estate was formally opened by King George VI on 22 February 1939 and construction continued during the war years.

50.   Team Valley – a study in straight lines with a series of horizontal and vertical edges formed by roadside kerbs, street lighting and sections of the bridge.

51. The premises of Tyneside Peeled Potatoes Ltd. on the Team Valley Trading Estate, showing a female employee at work.

52. Clarke Chapman's Victoria Works. The company was set up on the south shore in the early 1860s by William Clarke. Premises on St James' Road were acquired in 1874 and it was about this time that Captain William Chapman joined the company. Early work concentrated on the manufacture of winches but by the end of the 19th century boilers and electricity generating plants were being made.

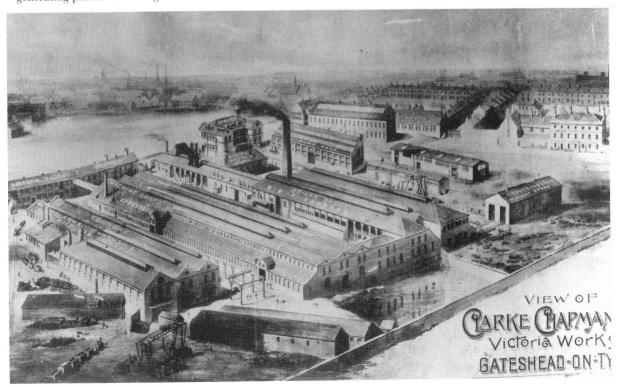

VIEW OF
CLARKE CHAPMAN
Victoria Works
GATESHEAD-ON-TY

53. Clarke Chapman's assembly shop. Claimed to be the biggest assembly works in Europe, it was equipped by Clarke Chapman, makers of steam generators for power stations, for building boilers under totally dust free conditions. In 1970 Clarke Chapman Ltd. merged with John Thomson of Wolverhampton.

Transport

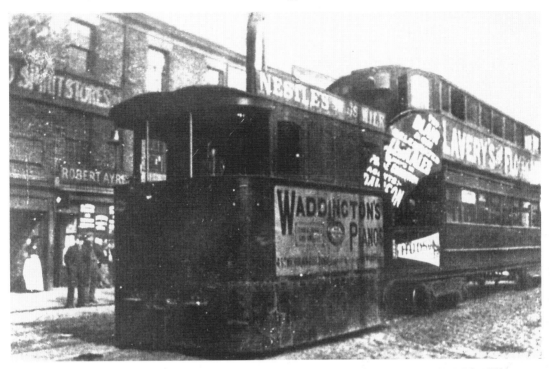

54. A steam engine and trailer built in 1883 for the tramway which operated from July 1883-May 1901, when electric trams took over the route.

55. A tram pictured in the early 1900s, with the maximum number of passengers on both decks.

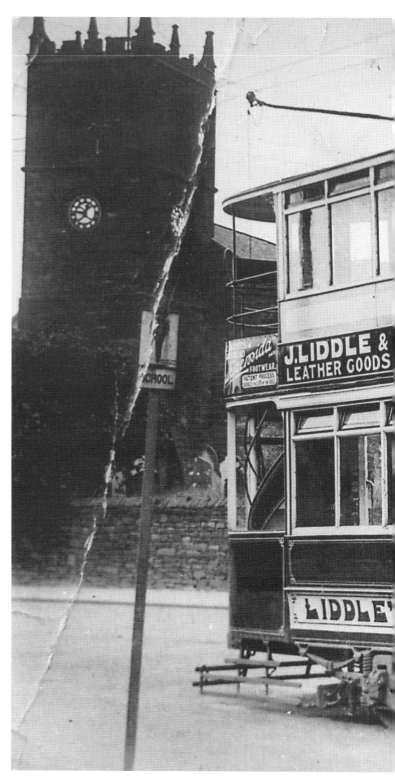

56. Heworth tram terminus. Driver Ferguson and conductor Scott are photographed in front of a tram which is well covered by advertisements for Liddle's leather products.

57. Gateshead tram staff. Third from the left is chief inspector Adam Armstrong and the driver is Sam Wilson.

58. A list of tram fares for Gateshead and District Tramways.

GATESHEAD and DISTRICT TRAMWAYS Co.
LIST OF FARES

HEWORTH		Fare	Stage No. Out	Stage No. In
Gateshead Station and	Claxton Hotel	1d.	1	4
Jackson Street "	Pear Tree Inn	1d.	2	3
Claxton Hotel "	Felling Station	1d.	3	2
Pear Tree "	Heworth Terminus	1d.	4	1
Gateshead Station "	Pear Tree Inn	1½d.	1	3
Sunderland R.E. "	Felling Station	1½d.	2	2
Claxton Hotel "	Heworth Terminus	1½d.	3	1
Gateshead Station "	Heworth Terminus	2d.	1	1

WREKENTON		Fare	Stage No. Out	Stage No. In
Gateshead Station and	Shipcote Terrace	1d.	1	5
Sunderland R.E. "	Pottery Lane	1d.	2	4
Shipcote Terrace "	Church Road	1d.	3	3
Pottery Lane "	Simpson's Cottages	1d.	4	2
Church Road "	Wrekenton	1d.	5	1
Gateshead Station "	Pottery Lane	1½d.	1	4
Sunderland R.E. "	Church Road	1½d.	2	3
Shipcote Terrace "	Simpson's Cottages	1½d.	3	2
Pottery Lane "	Wrekenton	1½d.	4	1
Gateshead Station "	Church Road	2d.	1	3
Sunderland R.E. "	Simpson's Cottages	2d.	2	2
Shipcote Terrace "	Wrekenton	2d.	3	1
Gateshead Station "	Simpson's Cottages	2½d.	1	2
Sunderland R.E. "	Wrekenton	2½d.	2	1
Gateshead Station "	Wrekenton	3d.	1	1

LOW FELL		Fare	Stage No. Out	Stage No. In
Gateshead Station and	Shipcote Terrace	1d.	1	4
Jackson Street "	Summerfield Road	1d.	2	3
Abbott School "	New Cannon Inn	1d.	3	2
Shipcote Terrace "	Low Fell Terminus	1d.	4	1
Gateshead Station "	New Cannon Inn	1½d.	1	2
Abbott School "	Low Fell Terminus	1½d.	2	1
Gateshead Station "	Low Fell Terminus	2d.	1	1

SALTWELL PARK		Fare	Stage No. Out	Stage No. In
Gateshead Station and	Bewick Road	1d.	1	2
St. Joseph's "	Saltwell Park	1d.	2	1
Gateshead Station "	Saltwell Park	1½d.	1	1

BENSHAM		Fare	Stage No. Out	Stage No. In
Gateshead Station and	Elysium Lane	1d.	1	2
Coatsworth R.E. "	Saltwell Cemetery	1d.	2	1
Gateshead Station "	Saltwell Cemetery	1½d.	1	1

DUNSTON		Fare	Stage No. Out	Stage No. In
Gateshead Station and	Pine St. (or Teams)	1d.	1	2
Redheugh Br. Rd. "	Dunston	1d.	2	1
Gateshead Station "	Dunston	1½d.	1	1

ALL TICKETS PUNCHED IN STAGE NUMBER WHERE PASSENGER BOARDS CAR.

WORKMEN'S FARES.
For Artisans, Mechanics and Daily Labourers.
Single Journey Tickets will be issued on all Cars up to 7 a.m. at 1d. for the full distance on each route, with the exception of Wrekenton where the fare will be:

WREKENTON ROUTE
1d. BETWEEN GATESHEAD STATION AND CHURCH ROAD
1d. " SUNDERLAND ROAD AND SIMPSON'S COTTAGES
1d. " SHIPCOTE TERRACE AND WREKENTON
1½d. " GATESHEAD STATION AND WREKENTON

WORKMEN COUPON TICKETS.
Artisans, Mechanics and Daily Labourers who wish to use Workmen's Coupon Tickets should complete an Application Form, which can be obtained at the Tramway Sub-office in Wellington Street Omnibus Station.

If the application is approved a Certificate will be issued enabling the holder to use Coupon Tickets. This Certificate must be produced when tickets are purchased and also on demand to any Inspector, Conductor or Servant of the Company.

These Tickets are available for travel up to 8 a.m., between 12 noon and 2.0 p.m., and between 4.0 and 6.30 p.m. (Saturdays excepted). They will not be available on Sundays and General Holidays and are not transferable.

Tickets are on Sale at WELLINGTON STREET OMNIBUS STATION at the following times :—

			Price of Coupon Tickets :—
Mondays & Fridays	From 12 noon to 1.0 p.m.		
" "	" 4 p.m. to 6.0 p.m.	Twelve 1d. Tickets - - -	1/-
Saturdays	" 12 noon to 6.0 p.m.	Twelve 1½d. Tickets - - -	1/6.

(BYE-LAW No. 12.)
"A passenger, not being an Artisan, Mechanic or Daily Labourer, within the true intent and meaning of the Acts of Parliament relating to the Company, shall not use or attempt to use any ticket intended only for such Artisans, Mechanics or Daily Labourers."

CHILDREN'S FARES
Children up to 3 years of age and not occupying a seat are carried free. From 3 to 12 years of age, Half Fare will be charged, with a minimum fare of 1d.
Children up to 15 years of age travelling to and from school are carried at half fare, provided they board the car before 4-30 p.m.

PASSENGER'S ACCOMPANIED LUGGAGE.
Passengers personal luggage, such as Handbags, Attache Cases, Bags of Tools, etc. up to 28lbs weight are carried free, subject to such articles being retained in the passengers' possession, and not occupying any portion of a seat or being of such a nature as to inconvenience any other passenger. All other articles of luggage must be placed on the platform of the car and will be charged for at the rate of 1d. per package on 1d. or 1½d. stages and 2d. per package for all other stages.

BULKY OR HEAVY ARTICLES LIKELY TO IMPEDE THE DRIVER OR CONDUCTOR, OR ARTICLES OF ANY OFFENSIVE NATURE, WILL NOT BE PERMITTED ON THE CAR UNDER ANY CIRCUMSTANCES.

The Company accepts no liability for Loss or Damage to Passengers' Accompanied Luggage, and the same is carried solely at owner's risk.

J. W. KING, Manager.

4.47. Robert Kelly, Ltd., Printers, West Street, Gateshead. F1656

59. A group of tram drivers and conductors on the Gateshead trams, photographed in 1940.

60. The Wellington Street approach to Gateshead railway station in the 1920s. The entrance to the High Level bridge (opened in 1849) is in the background and the arch on the right leads through to the Pipewellgate area.

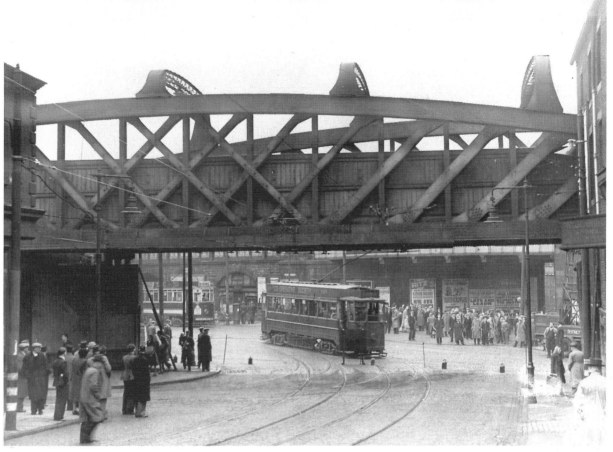

61. Railway bridge in West Street. The bridge had a total weight of 250 tons. Weekend work during May 1948 raised the structure by 2 ft. 6 ins. thus enabling double-decker buses to run under it.

62. North Eastern Railway goods yard at the corner of Eldon Street and Prior Street, photographed in 1964.

63.   A group of North Eastern Railway staff at a local station, *c*.1910.

64. A 'big city traffic hold-up' on 9 July 1951. An assortment of vehicles are pictured close to the High Level bridge during the biggest traffic jam seen on Tyneside for some 18 years. It occurred largely as a result of the closure of the Redheugh bridge.

65.   The first section of the £½ million Gateshead-Felling bypass in May 1959. On the left of the photograph are Pelaw railway station and the C.W.S. factory at Pelaw.

Schools and Schooldays

66.   Gateshead Grammar School. The school was opened in 1883 as a Municipal Higher Grade school, and demolished in November 1963. Built to 'supply the rising manhood of Tyneside district' on a site close to the Shipley Art Gallery, the school had an open view of Saltwell Park when it was first completed. By 1890 the premises had been extended to accommodate 540 pupils.

67.   The Health school on Joicey Road, Low Fell, was opened on 29 June 1937 by the mayor, Alderman J. White.

68. Kelvin Grove school pictured in April 1989 shortly before demolition work got underway. During May 1990, however, fire swept through the building before contractors had completed demolition. When the school opened in 1902 it was occupied by junior and infant classes.

69. John Kelly pictured outside Prior Street junior school which opened in 1874.

70. A mixed class of pupils at Prior Street school in 1914. The photographer has asked them to pose with hands clasped in front of them on the desk top. It is interesting to compare wall displays, lighting and general layout of this classroom with those of the 1990s.

71. Standard VII pupils at Prior Street school in 1927-28, photographed outside the boys' entrance. The teacher, Mr. Finney, does not appear on this occasion.

72. Miss Smith's class at Corpus Christi school, Dunsmuir Grove, in 1949. The school building made headlines shortly after opening in 1909 when it was struck by lightning. Then for nearly 20 years it served as a church for the people of Bensham and Saltwell. On the 60th anniversary of the building's opening a celebration mass was held, and the parish priest, Father Patrick McKenna was, was assisted on the altar by 14 priests, all former pupils of the school.

73. Carol Lytollis returns home via the back gate after a day at school in 1950. The family lived in Westbourne Avenue, Gateshead, and were well-known locally.

74. Brighton Avenue school pupils photographed in 1909. The school was opened in 1894.

75. Alexandra Road schools opened in 1875.

76. Pupils in the yard of Whitehall Road school in the early 1950s. The school was opened on 30 October by the Rt. Hon. A. J. Mundella. At the opening the architect spoke of his desire to provide a good, plain, workmanlike building, well lit and ventilated and with light adapted to scientific principles so that it came in from the left of the child at work.

Street Scenes and Housing Development

77. Bowl Alley Bank leading to Pipewellgate, photographed in 1886. Occupants of properties on the left of the picture sold fish (upper level) and vegetables (lower level) at the local market.

78. Pipewellgate in 1886 looking in an easterly direction towards the medieval core of the town. This passage was 8ft. wide and had along each side slum housing, small workshops and one or two shops.

79. St Mary's church viewed from the High Level bridge. Most of the church building dates from the 14th century, although the tower is of 18th-century construction. Earlier buildings on the site were badly damaged by fire in 1080 and 1854, and the present structure was also struck by fire on 19 October 1979. It was deconsecrated and after facing an uncertain future it was handed over to Phillips Fine Art Auctioneers in November 1990.

80. Church Street in the 1920s. St Mary's church occupies a central position in the picture.

81. Bridge Street in 1924.

82. Church Street in 1930.

83. Bottle Bank, with a ship passing through the Swing Bridge. The street is probably of Anglo-Saxon derivation – 'Botl' refers to a house or dwelling. The Swing Bridge was opened in 1876. It measures about 280 ft. in length, and is still operated by its original hydraulic system with power from electric pumps.

84. Amen Corner, at the junction of the old High Street West and Gladstone Street, *c.*1925. The presence of three churches, United Free Methodist church, Bellevue Terrace, Baptist church, Gladstone Terrace, and Presbyterian church, Durham Road, gave rise to the name Amen Corner. Much of this area was demolished in the 1950s and '60s to make way for the Gateshead highway.

85.   Durham Road, Low Fell, photographed *c*.1900.

86.   Pipewellgate in 1927, showing Brett's works and offices which were at the bottom right-hand corner. Brett's handled oils, petroleum distribution and did oil refining on a small scale.

87. Shop premises on Saltwell Road owned by M. Sober, photographed in 1976.

88. Pine Street pictured in the summer of 1973 shortly before demolition work got underway. Pine Street was cleared as part of slum clearance schemes and to make way for a new road.

89. Demolition work behind West Street was undertaken as part of the Metro Station development.

90. Terraced properties in Derwentwater Road.

91. Avenue Road, photographed in 1973.

BELLE VUE BANK

92. Belle Vue Bank, photographed from Durham Road in 1961. The picture shows the Low Fell district looking down towards Team Valley.

93. Beacon Lough estate, between Sheriff Hill and Wrekenton, photographed in summer 1952. Between 1945-50 a total of 1,293 houses were completed at the Lobley Hill and Beacon Lough estates along with other dwellings at Wrekenton and Lyndhurst where building work continued until the 1950s. The beacon referred to in the estate's name was one of a series of warning beacons set up in the reign of Queen Elizabeth I.

94. Lobley Hill district with the Hillheads secondary modern school on the extreme left of the photograph, which was taken in the early 1960s. Team Valley is on the extreme right.

95. Newly-built council houses at Easdale Gardens, Lyndhurst estate, photographed in August 1971.

96. A stone arch on Sheriff Hill. It used to lead into Anderson Place, Pilgrim Street, Newcastle, the home of Major Anderson. When the Anderson estate was bought by Richard Grainger for redevelopment the arch was moved to Sheriff Hill and used as the entrance gate to the new rectory of Gateshead Fell church.

Saltwell Park

97. The 58-acre Saltwell Park was landscaped for public use in 1877 and, although some of the early features have gone, it still provides an ideal venue for family outings. Saltwell Towers, a large brick-built mansion, was constructed between 1860-71 for the Tyneside glass manufacturer, William Wailes. During the years following the Second World War the mansion was used as a local and industrial museum but it is now derelict. This picture shows the salt well which gave the park its name and which was renowned for its healing properties.

98. Saltwell Park in 1920 with Saltwell Towers dominating the landscaped area. Yellow and black materials highlighted the red brickwork while turrets, chimneys and battlements added a touch of Victorian grandeur.

99. Saltwell Towers with its prominent towers and
chimney stacks.

100. The interior of Saltwell Towers. Constructed during
1860-71 for William Wailes, it contained a range of
extravagant fittings and furniture.

101. A wooden sculpture from Saltwell Park. The carving of Robinson Crusoe from a block of white pine was completed by Gerald Robinson in 1862. Even the parrot in the cage was fashioned from the same piece of wood.

102. Carvings from the mansion in Saltwell Park. These depict scenes from the action at the battle of Chevy Chase and are the work of Gerald Robinson, who created a sensation at the 1851 Crystal Palace Exhibition with his Chevy Chase sideboard carving.

103. The sign for the *Goat Inn* was made by the Newcastle carver Gerald Robinson. The name Gateshead originally referred to a headland or hill on which goats roamed on Felling and Windy Nook. An inn at the top of Bottle Bank was renamed *Goat Inn* c.1650. The golden goat from the old *Goat Inn* is shown here on display in Saltwell Park museum. It is now housed in the Shipley Art Gallery on Prince Consort Road.

104. An item from the museum at Saltwell – this hall stand, made from the wood of a mulberry tree, was one of three presented by King James I to the Sheriff of Newcastle to encourage the development of the silk industry in the north. One tree stood in the grounds of the Brandlings at Felling and was cut down to make furniture.

105. A kiosk from 1929 which was removed from the North East Coast Exhibition in Newcastle to Saltwell Park for use as a rest room.

106. Saltwell Park's ornate drinking fountain.

107.   Saltwell Park lake pictured in 1904.

108.   Saltwell Park bandstand. After being sited in several locations in the park, including a position in the middle of the park, the bandstand was moved to Beamish North of England Open Air Museum.

109. Model yacht club members on a visit to Saltwell Park pictured at the turn of the century.

110. Carol and Eileen Lytollis photographed during 1948 in one of the decorative turrets in the lake close to Saltwell Towers.

111. Brenda Lamb pictured with her parents, Willa and Jack, on a park bench in Saltwell Park in 1948.

112. Eileen Lytollis, Brenda Lamb and Carol Lytollis, photographed beside Saltwell Park lake in 1949.

Local People

THE TYNESIDE AREA of north-east England has its own unique culture. Evolved in workplaces and communities on either side of the river – and best known for dialect words and phrases – it blends enterprise and initiative with humour and warmth of character.

Tynesiders or 'Geordies' have achieved success in many walks of life but the spirit and dynamism of this area is probably best summed up in scenes from the everyday lives of some Gateshead families.

113. William Errington Kelly and his wife Sabina Anthony Reed (née Leonard). Mr. Kelly was born on 23 December 1874 at 32 Broughton Place, Newcastle-upon-Tyne and died on 13 March 1959 at Bensham hospital. Mrs. Kelly was born on 9 October 1879 at Custom House Quay, Shadwell Street, South Shields and died on 21 January 1957 at Queen Elizabeth Hospital, Sheriff Hill, Gateshead.

114. Mother and sons. Sabina Kelly with George aged 5½ and John aged six months, photographed in 1906.

115. George and John Kelly, photographed in 1909 outside 23 Eldon Street.

116. Bina Kelly (aged 14), Willa Kelly (aged 12) and Bina Nuttall (aged two), photographed in 1922.

117. A day out for the Kelly and Lytollis families, 1934.

118. Sisters Bina and Willa Kelly, aged 17 and 15, photographed in 1935 during a camping holiday on land adjacent to a watercourse known locally as The Gut. The area is now covered by Team Valley and the river which is a tributary of the Tyne runs under the main road.

119. Bernard Kelly, brother of Willa, was a local businessman and trader. He is pictured here in 1934.

120. The Kelly family during an outing to Ravensworth in 1936. From left to right, top: Willa Kelly, Louisa, Bina; below: brother Bernard, Joe Lytollis, Walter.

121. Ravensworth Castle. The oldest sections of the castle date from the 13th and 14th centuries. In recent years it has had a succession of owners. Much of the fabric has now been demolished due to damage caused by subsidence. It was a favoured place for local families to visit.

122.   The gateway to Ravensworth Castle.

123.   Walter Nuttall was brother-in-law of Willa Kelly. He was
an expert on various breeds of dogs and officiated at Crufts Dog
Show. This picture dates from 1939.

124. Sabina and William Errington Kelly pictured with a 1935 Morris 8 outside *Waggon Team Inn* in 1939. *Waggon Team Inn* opened in 1938 as development of the Team Valley continued. A *Waggon Inn* had stood in Gateshead High Street, close to Burton the Tailor premises, and, following its demolition, the licence was transferred to the new premises shown here.

125. Willa Kelly pictured in August 1938. A keen cyclist and motorbike rider, she is pictured wearing her leather gauntlets.

126.   Atlas Stone football team, pictured in the 1930s.

127. Jack and Willa Lamb on their wedding day, 7 March 1942. During the Second World War he served in the Navy and Willa was a member of the W.A.A.F.

128. *(above)* Brenda Lamb is pictured here, in 1946, in her pram outside 119 Woodbine Street, then the premises of a general dealer.

129. *(above right)* A trio of local men, 'The Jolly Boys', are pictured in Whitehall Road in 1947. On the left is Jack Lamb, next to him is Bernard Kelly, and on the right, Albert Sadler, who worked at the Whitehall Cooperative Stores.

130. *(right)* William Errington Kelly, photographed in 1950, close to his Highfield Road home, holding cups he had won for breeding pigeons. A wood machinist by trade and father of Willa Kelly, he achieved local fame after selling a prize pigeon to King George V.

131. Brenda Lamb and Margaret Taylor pictured at a dancing class in the Cooperative Hall, Whitehall Road on 1 July 1951. Miss Mullen was the dancing teacher.

132. Pictured opposite the Cooperative Society premises in Whitehall Road are (from left to right): Diane Burrell, Margaret Taylor, Brenda Lamb, Hilderic Best and Jane Burnall. Hair ribbons seem to have been the order of the day as part of young ladies' hairstyles in 1951.

133. A family day out at Ravensworth in 1952. Brenda Lamb is pictured with her mother, father, grandmother and Uncle George.

134. Hearses are drawn up in Brussel Streeet, Teams, for the funeral of Sabina Kelly in 1955. Brick-built terraces were a feature of this area of Gateshead, with stone being used for lintels and kerbstones.

135. Alexander Gillies, Mayor of Gateshead 1900-2 and 1906-7, of Ravensworth Terrace.

136. Shipcote Villas, *c*.1900. The Dance family lived in the front section of no. 2. The building was demolished in the late 1920s or early 1930s.

137. 2 Shipcote Villa, the master bedroom, photographed *c*.1900.

138.   The library at Shipcote Villa, *c*.1900.

139.   The drawing room at Shipcote Villa, *c*.1900.

140. Helen and Henzel Dance, photographed in 1910 at 2 Shipcote Villa. They are dressed for a dance and pose for the camera in the conservatory.

141.   The Dance family in a horse-drawn brake cart in the yard of their house, *c.*1900.

142. Local people on an outing. Headwear seems to be compulsory for this photograph. The fourth child from the right on the second row is Maria Neville (née Hewitt) sitting on the knee of her mother, Ellen Hewitt (née Troy).

143.   Members of the Home Guard with dispatch riders at Burt Terrace in 1940.

144.   The Gateshead battalion of the Boys Brigade at Woodhorn camp in 1906. The Rev. Rhodes is addressing the lads.

145. Members of the Gateshead battalion of the Boy Scouts photographed at the crossroads, Ravensworth, on Whit Monday 1909.

146. Harrison's Slipway staff, Matthew Bonner, Ted Smith, Billy Butler and Ken Taylor solved an engine problem on the German sailing ship *Monsun* two days before the Cutty Sark race. The company announced plans to restore the 166-year-old repair yard and return to building boats.

Social Life

147. A postcard from Gateshead of 1933 showing St Mary's, the town's mother church, and popular locations for family outings – Saltwell Park and Ravensworth Castle.

148. The Essoldo Cinema was also known as the Alhambra, Kings and Empire Theatre. It was built in 1905 on a site bordering Sunderland Road. It closed as a theatre on 29 April 1950, re-opening the following day as a cinema. However, it continued to stage professional Christmas pantomimes until 1965. It finally closed on 30 December 1967 and was demolished in 1968 to make way for road improvements.

149. Palace Cinema was built in 1911 and demolished in 1963. It was situated on Romsey High Street, High Spen.

150. Coatsworth Picture Hall on Bewick Road opened in 1913 and had a seating capacity of 1,342. It closed in August 1960 and re-opened as a bingo hall in 1963.

151. Rex Cinema, photographed in 1939. It was built in Askew Road West in 1939 and had a seating capacity of 1,022. It became a bingo hall in 1961 and was demolished in 1973.

152.　The publican and regulars pose for a photograph in their public house in the Salt Meadows area of Gateshead.

153. *Beacon Hotel*, photographed in June 1962. The new style public houses of the 1960s and '70s form a clear contrast with earlier downtown inns.

154. The newly opened *Norwood Hotel*, photographed on 10 December 1965.

155. *Plough Inn* at Deckham. It replaced an old public house of the same name. The new building was said to be typical of the new style of licensed premises with an off-sales section and neat brickwork, doors and windows. The picture was taken in December 1967.

Local Events

156.   Ann Carr, a miner's wife and resident of Friar's Goose, is evicted from her home after shouting 'Union for ever' whilst the local men are forcibly restrained by officers of the law. These events of 4 May 1832 became known as 'The Battle of Friar's Goose'.

157.   On 8 May 1832 the part owner and manager of Friar's Goose collieries led policemen in an attempt to persuade rebellious pitmen that the cottages they lived in belonged to the colliery. He pointed out that if they did not work they had no right to occupy the cottages. This engraving shows pitmen encamped in temporary shelters having been evicted from their cottages.

158. Newton Street in 1902. Young and old
gather under a variety of flags and banners at
a celebration which probably marked the
return of soldiers from the Boer War. It was
also the coronation year for King Edward
VII.

159. A bonfire under construction at
Shadon's Hill near Birtley to mark the
coronation of King Edward VII.

160. Officers and men march through the streets of Gateshead during a local army parade in 1906. St Joseph's church is in the background.

161. A V.E. party in Westbourne Avenue, May 1945. Bunting has been spread across this road of terraced properties and tables and chairs are set up along the roadway as residents celebrate the Allies' victory in Europe over Axis forces (the alliance of Nazi Germany, Fascist Italy and Japan). Willa Lamb is on the left of the picture and Bina Lytollis on the front right.

162.   Children from Camborne Grove and Whitehall Road celebrate the coronation of Queen Elizabeth II on 2 June 1953. Many of them are in fancy dress as they gather round the carnival queen in the Whitehall Road Cooperative Hall.

163.   A group of boys with flags await the arrival of the festival queen during celebrations at Corpus Christi school, Brighton Road, in 1953.

164. Festival queen and attendants pictured at Corpus Christi school during celebrations in 1953.

165. An assortment of uniforms and fancy dress is on show outside the entrance to the infants department of Corpus Christi school on Empire Day 1953.

166. Gateshead's mayor, Councillor Bob Rudge, unveils a plaque at the Dispensary building on Nelson Street at a ceremony on 12 October 1982.

167. The Dunston end of the Garden Festival site showing three bridges across the Tyne, the Newcastle Tyne Valley and Carlisle railway (at the top of the photograph) and the Rocket block of flats to the right.

168. The National Festival 1990. Opened by the Princess Royal in May 1990, the site included more than 100 gardens or garden features. These ranged from a wetlands garden, devised by the Northumberland Wildlife Trust, to a display of municipal gardens from Harrogate. This photograph shows a spaceship-shaped pavilion which was staffed during the festival by staff from Gateshead libraries and arts.

169. National Garden Festival site. The south-western sector of the site was dominated by the giant outline of the ferris wheel.

170.   The Garden Festival site. Contrasting modes of transport around the site included a traditional Tyneside tramcar, road-train, and the futuristic monorail system; an obvious favourite with younger visitors, which is photographed passing the dramatic assembly of sculptures known as the *Red Army*.

171.   The Garden Festival site. The northern end of the site sloped down to the River Tyne. Pictured here is the riverside road-train station and 19th-century coaling staiths. The staiths, restored as part of the festival, were originally used to load coal ships for transportation to London and the south of England.

172. Brendan Foster celebrates victory after the International Cross Country event at Gateshead Riverside Bowl in 1975.

173. Action from the Schweppes International cross country team race on 25 November 1978. The field is led by no. 1, Bernie Ford, and no. 4, Dave Black.

174. Gateshead's mayor presents Jill Hunter with the spoils of victory after the Trophy Run at Gateshead International stadium in 1984.

175. Two of the best known figures in world athletics during recent years, American athletes Ed Moses and Florence Joyner at the Gateshead stadium in 1988.

176.   A view along one of the shopping malls in the Metro Centre which covers three and a half miles of land. The complex includes Metroland, which is Europe's only indoor theme park, a 10-screen multiplex cinema and a 10-pin bowling centre.

177.   The Metro Centre was developed on reclaimed land three miles from the centre of Gateshead. Plans for the scheme were announced in 1982, work started two years later and the first store was trading by April 1986 – with most of the shops opening six months later. Some 360 shops are included in the layout, which represents Europe's largest out-of-town shopping and leisure complex.